Creative Guitar Mastery: Movable Chord Workbook

j. Christian Miller

A book in the Creative Guitar Mastery™ series

International Standard Serial Number:

ISSN 1545-8385 (print)
ISSN 1545-8393(online)

Conceived, Written, & Illustrated by Chris Miller.

The Creative Guitar Mastery™ Series
1332 Cat Gap
Clayton, Georgia 30525

Phone: 1-706-982-5522
Web: www.CreativeGuitarMastery.com

Creative Guitar Mastery™ and CreativeGuitarMastery.com are imprints of DoublePlanet.com Publishing & Consultation

Library of Congress Control Number: 2013911294

International Standard Serial Number (ISSN):
ISSN 1545-8385 (print)
ISSN 1545-8407(CD-ROM)
ISSN 1545-8393(online)

International Standard Book Number (ISBN):
Creative Guitar Mastery: Moveable Chord Workbook
(Print) ISBN: 978-0-9743571-5-7
Creative Guitar Mastery: Movable Chord Workbook
(Electronic) ISBN: 978-0-9743571-6-4
Creative Guitar Mastery: Movable Chord Workbook
(iTunes iBookstore) ISBN: 978-0-9743571-7-1

Table Of Contents

Introduction

Who is this for?

This book is dedicated to the creative guitarist. It is aimed at the person seeking to further develop their understanding of how to use this wonderful instrument to express themselves in their own unique way. It is for the person in the rock band, the singer/songwriter plunking out chords and melodies to go along with their words. It is for the guy out in the garage spending hours on end honing the craft of recording music on his computer. It is for anyone trying to find his or her unique creative voice and express it through the medium of the guitar.

This book is aimed at the student who pursues music from a creative viewpoint. It is especially for the person trying to get a grip on movable chords. It is not full of theory. In fact, there is a minimum of instruction included.

Why was it written?

Movable Chord Workbook was written to give you the quickest path to the most complete understanding of movable chords on the guitar. You could spend a small fortune in tuition and rent, move to Boston and go to a fancy private college and study guitar and music theory for years while they trickle it out over years and years.

I wrote it in an attempt to fill the gaps in the information available to the student of creative guitar who is seeking to tune-in to their own unique creative voices. There is a lot of information here. Hopefully, the sheer volume of all that's here will not overwhelm the mindful student.

Instead, I hope that you will keep a copy of this book around for years to come and refer back to it every now and then to realize how much the material here can transform your playing as the ideas take root in your mind.

How was it written?

I tried to make the smallest, yet most complete chord book possible. Therefore, I omitted the instruction for the book to a bare minimum. It is simply a movable chord workbook. There are lots of chords books out there, but this one is simpler, leading to more complete understanding.

Use the book as a reference, to complete your understanding, and especially application of movable chords.

When and where was it written?

This book is the result of over twenty years of serious pursuit of guitar mastery especially as an instrument to express my own creativity in the form of being a songwriter and most importantly, a creative guitarist.

Early on I realized that if you wanted to study guitar from a creative standpoint, or as a means to express your own creativity, and to interact with other such people to create music that was uniquely your own and no one else's a more holistic approach was needed.

This material is geared toward this creative philosophy. It is for the guitarist trying to get a practical grip on movable chords.

What does it cover?

The workbook gives the most complete picture of useable chords in the smallest space. The book conveys a limited set of chords. It is the most common, most graspable set of movable chords. You could get through just about any gig with this set of chords.

The most basic way to know your moveable chord forms is to be able play each of them in common cycles. The most common cycles are descending and ascending 5ths. Check out this pictorial diagram of this type of chord motion.

Go counter-clockwise for resolving 5ths. The other way is ascending 5ths. Be able to go either way with these forms individually. This is a good place to start.

The Cycle of 5ths

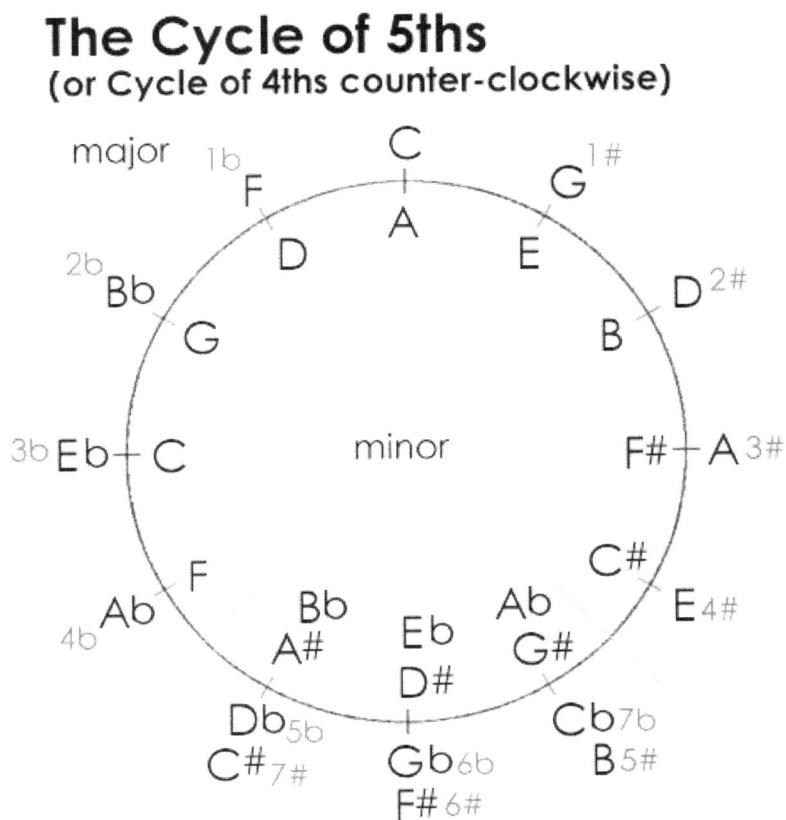

The Cycle of 5ths
(or Cycle of 4ths counter-clockwise)

major 1b   C   1#
  F | G
      A
  2b   E
 Bb   D 2#
  G   B

minor

3b Eb─C   F#─A 3#

  F   C#
 4b Ab Bb   Ab E 4#
    A# Eb G#
        D#
   Db 5b   Cb 7b
  C# 7# Gb 6b B 5#
       F# 6#

Order of sharps (#): F C G D A E B
Order of flats (b): B E A D G C F

Chords are organized by what string their root is on, and also by related shapes. This is the most logical order for a book. However, it would behoove the student to learn them in a practical way. See supplements to this book for more ideas here.

Basic Forms

6th String Root

E Form

13

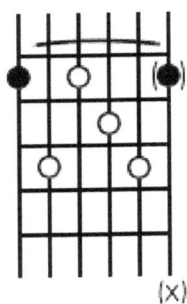

(x)

13

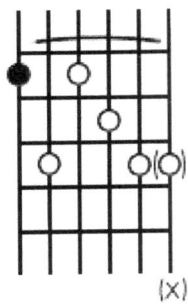

(x)

13sus4

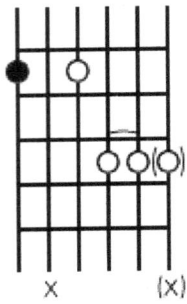

x   (x)

mi

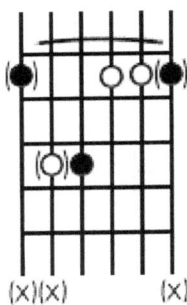

(x)(x)   (x)

mi7

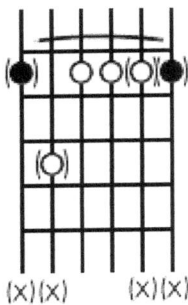

(x)(x)   (x)(x)

mi9

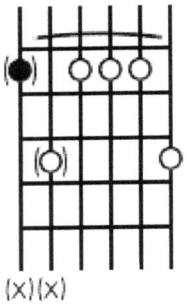

(x)(x)

mi7

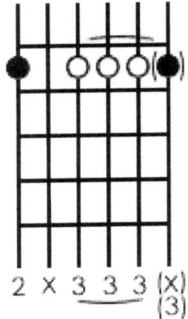

2 X 3 3 3 (X)
            (3)

mi9

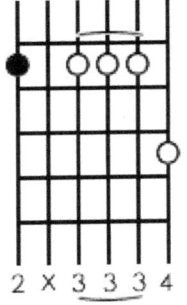

2 X 3 3 3 4

mi6

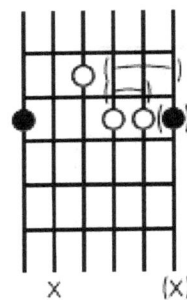

x   (x)

mi7b5

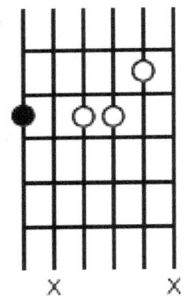

x   x

dim7 (o7)

x   x

6

G Form

| major | 6 | ma6(9) | 9b5 | 7#5#9 |

Line Clichés

Line cliches are those groovy little chord changes that involve one line moving among a set of common notes. Check these out.

| (major) | ma7 | 7 | 6 |

And another.

| mi | mi(ma7) | mi7 | mi6 |

A Form

mi7

major

```
 2  X  3  3  (X)        (X)        (X)
              (3)
```

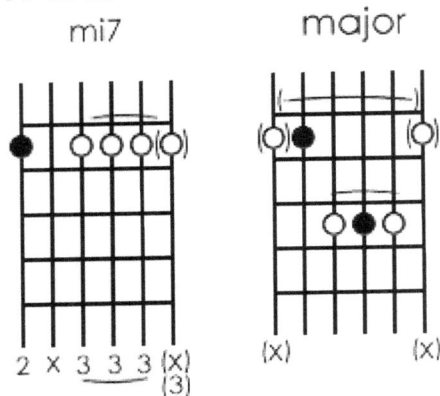

This form is related elsewhere to the E form. It is also related to the A shape with its root on the 5th string. In Jazz, oftentimes the IV chord is replaced by the ii mi chord. This is the same type of thinking as this relationship between these two chords. For example, in the key of G Major, the IV chord is C Major. The ii mi chord is Ami. The mi7 form of this would be Ami7. Compare these to get the full picture of this thinking.

Assumed Root

Assumed root chords are chords whose root is not actually in the chord. Rely on your bassist and or other rhythm section players to fill in the roots, etc. these are some far out chords for us old school rockers. But they really add a new dimension to your playing. Learn them to add new twists to what you already know. Or learn them to fill in your jazz chord knowledge. Or even for the physical workout of building dexterity!

This is a lot of information. Take little bites and chew them well. Give the, time to digest. You might learn one or two of these shapes at a time.

Root 5th String

A Form

major

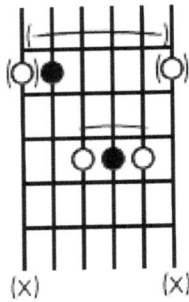

(ma)6

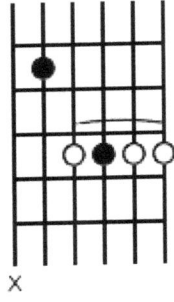

ma7

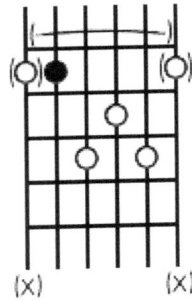

7

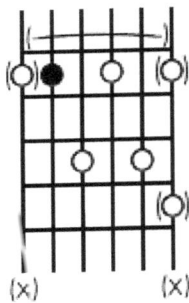

7sus4

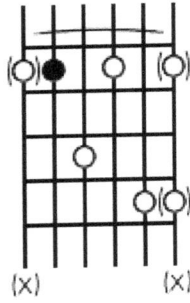

11(or 9sus4)

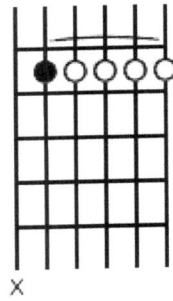

7sus4

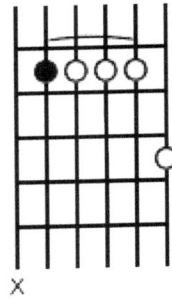

7#5

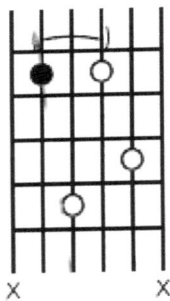

7b5

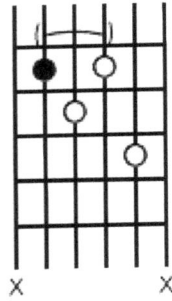

mi	mi7	mi7b5	o7 or dim7
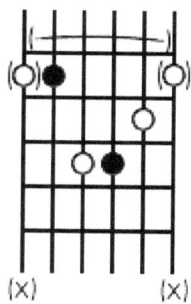	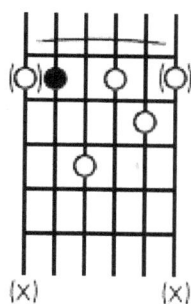	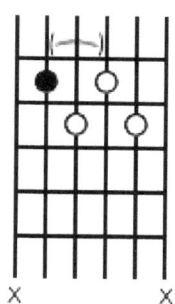	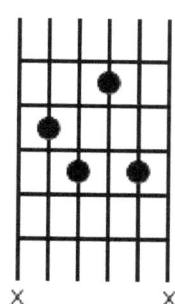

C Form

(major)	ma7	(ma)6	ma⁹₆	ma⁹₇
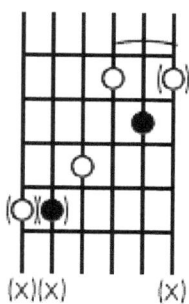	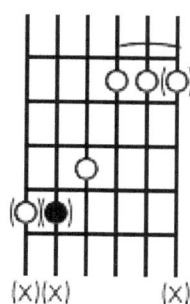	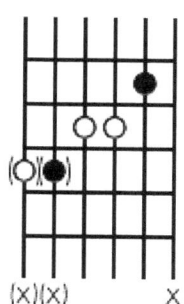	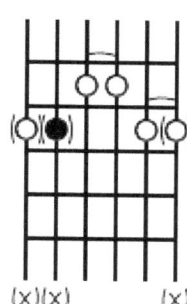	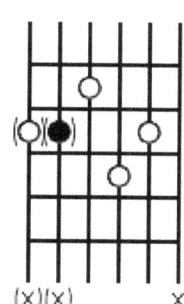

7	9	13
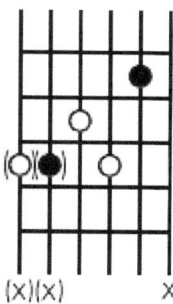	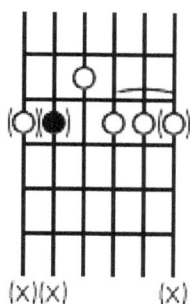	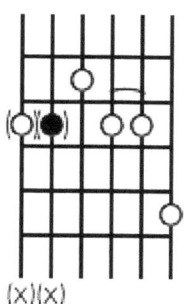

9
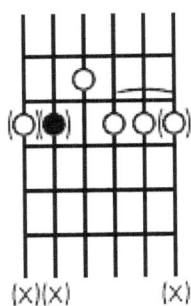

9#5
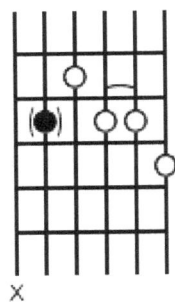

7#5b9
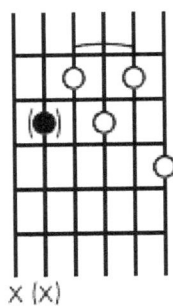

7b9
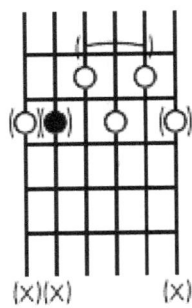

7#9
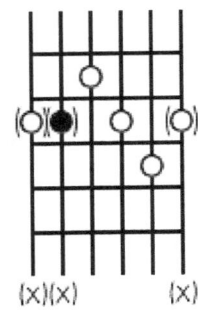

7b5b9
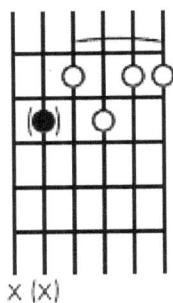

minor
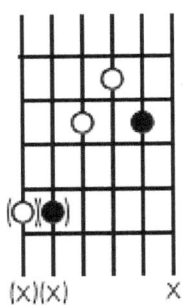

mi7
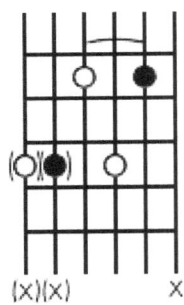

mi9
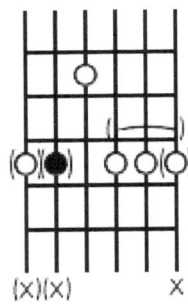

aug or +
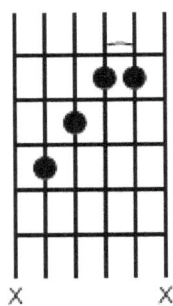

aug add9
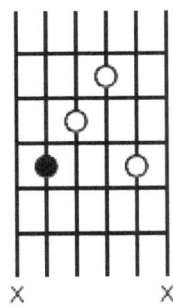

Line Clichés

mi, mi(ma7),   mi, mi+5, mi6   mi, mi+5, mi6
mi7, mi6

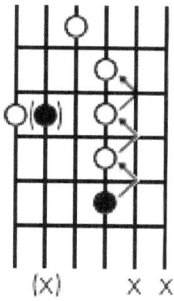 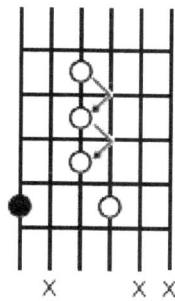 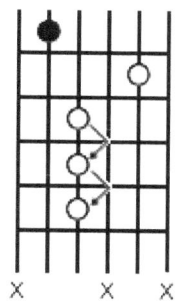

mi   mi(ma7)   mi7   mi6

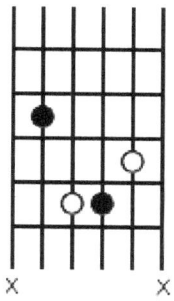 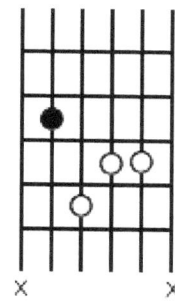 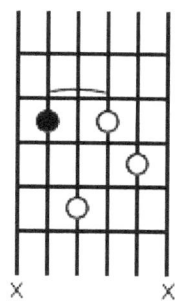 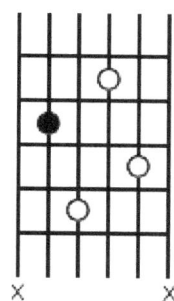

mi   mi(ma7)   mi7   mi6

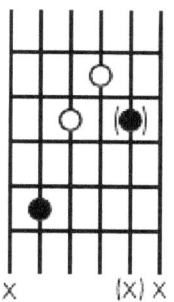 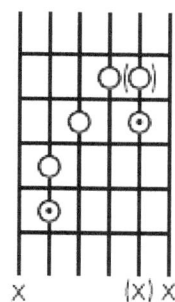 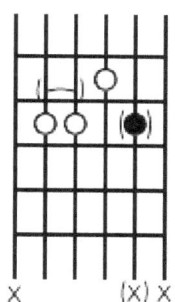 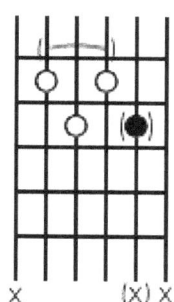

Assumed Root

7♭9

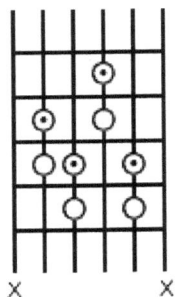

Root 4ᵗʰ String

D Form

7	mi6	dim7(o or o7)

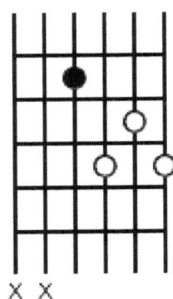 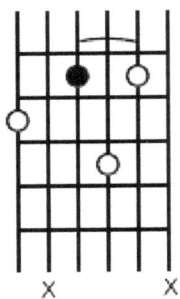 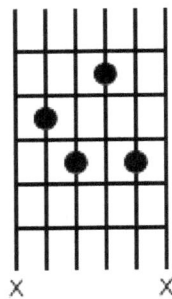

F Form

(major)	(ma)6	ma7

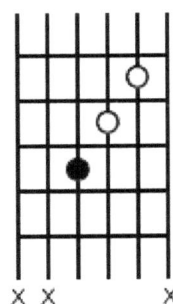 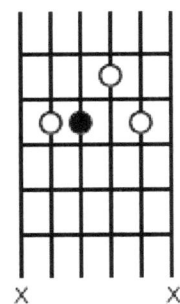 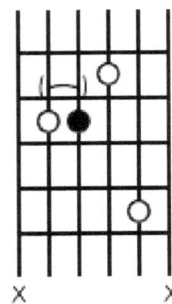

7
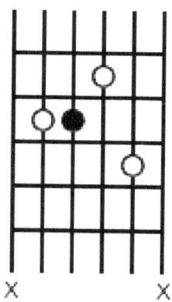

7b5
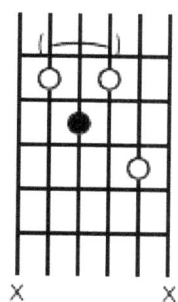

7#5
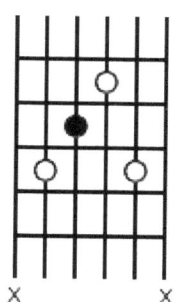

aug or +
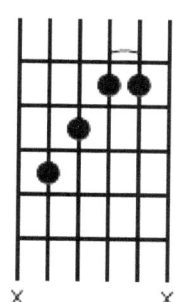

mi
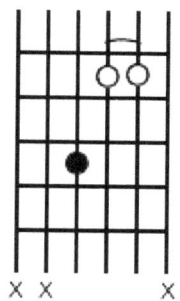

mi6
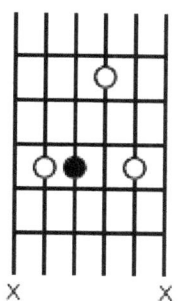

mi7
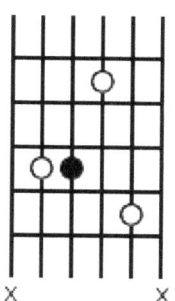

mi7b5
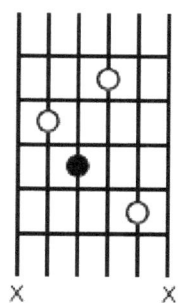

dim7 (o or o7)
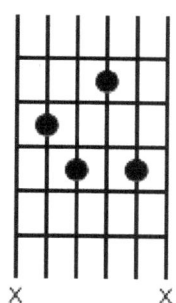

Assumed Root

7♭9

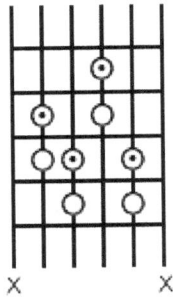

Root 3rd String

G Form

(dom)7

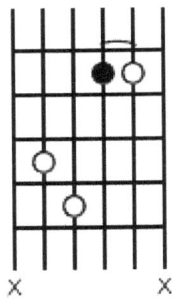

6

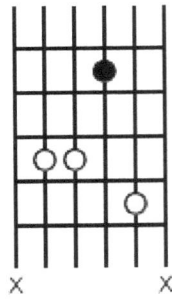

13

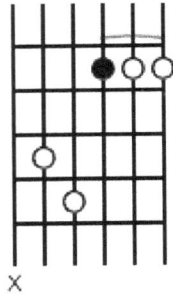

mi6

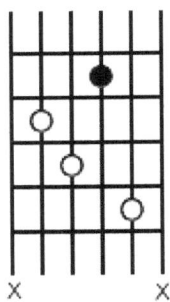

mi6

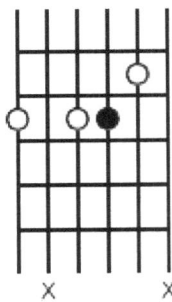

aug or +

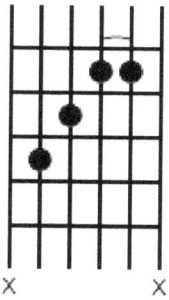

The above augmented chord is symmetrical. The result is that each note in the chord can serve as the chord's root. This also results in the fact that each chord repeats every four frets.

Another example of this the diminished 7 chord.

dim7 (o or o7)

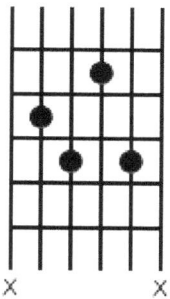

Assumed Root

7b9

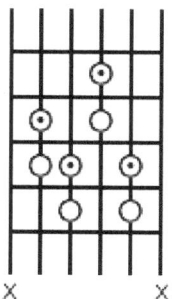

Root 2nd String

D Form

mi6   mi7b5   dim7(o or o7)

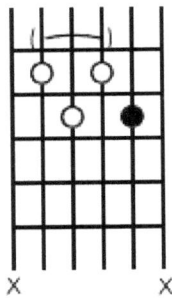 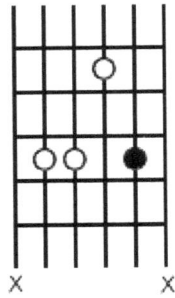 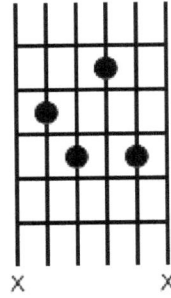

C Form

7   13   7sus4

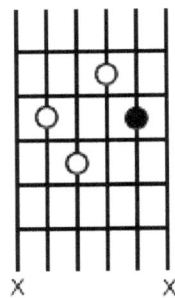 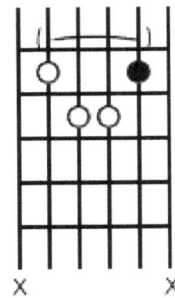 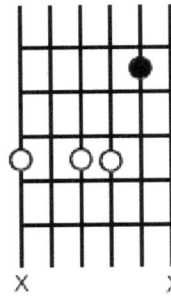

7b5   7b5   7#5

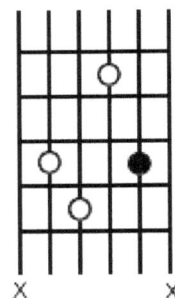 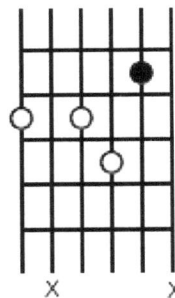 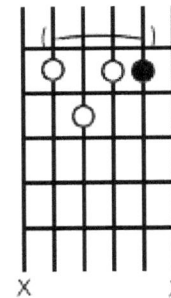

mi7   mi6

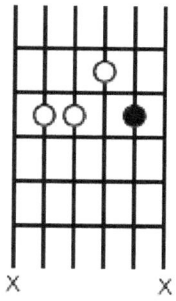 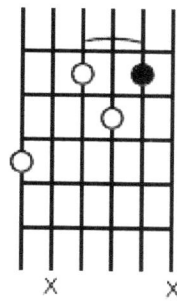

mi7b5   dim7(o or o7)

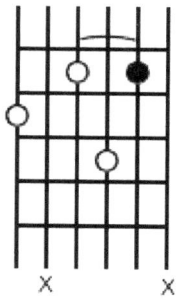 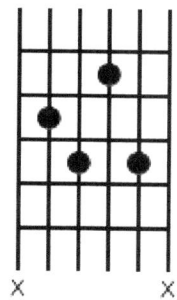

Line Cliché

mi, mi+5, mi6

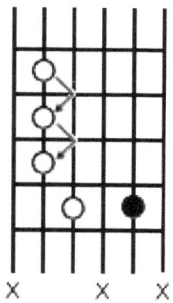

Assumed Root

9   13   13b9

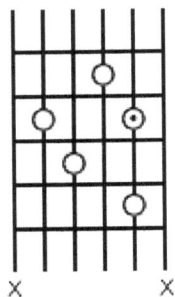 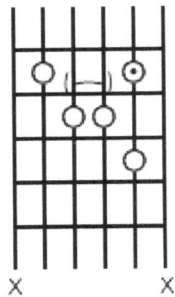 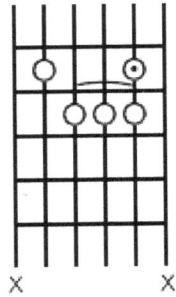

9#5   7#9#5   9b5

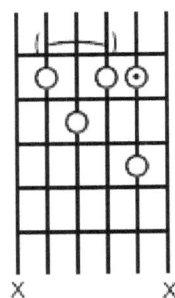 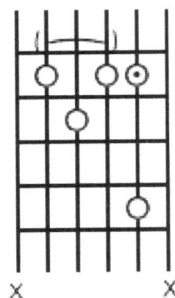 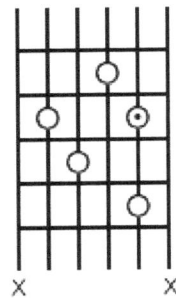

7b9   7b9   7b9b5   7b9#5

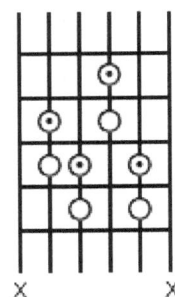 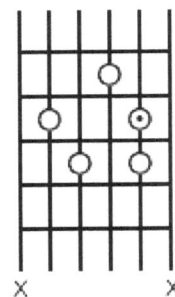 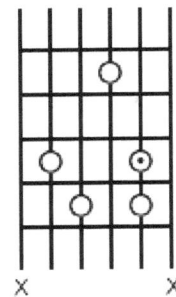 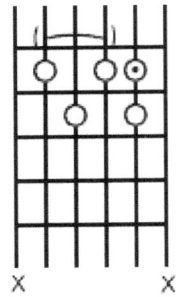

Appendix

Chord formulas, 7th Chords:

ma7 = R, 3, 5, 7

(dominant)7 = R, 3, 5, b7

mi7 = R, b3, 5, b7

mi7(b5) = R, b3, b5, b7

o7 (diminished7) = R, b3, b5, bb7

ma7+ (major7 augmented, or ma7+5) = R, 3, #5, 7

mi(ma)7 = R, b3, 5, 7

What Next?

The Creative Guitar Mastery™ Series is college-level learning geared toward that special learner trying to nurture your own unique creative voice through the practice of creative guitar. This learning offers top-down, thorough, and practical knowledge leading toward a complete mastery of the guitar as a creative instrument.

the Creative Guitar Mastery™ series
ISSN (International Standard Serial Number) Information
Creative Guitar Mastery (print) ISSN 1545-8385
Creative Guitar Mastery (CD) ISSN 1545-8407
Creative Guitar Mastery (online electronic) ISSN 1545-8393

The Creative Guitar Mastery Series
www.CreativeGuitarMastery.com
an imprint of DoublePlanet.com
1332 Cat Gap Clayton, Georgia 30525
Web: www.DoublePlanet.com
E-mail: chris@doubleplanet.com
Phone: 1-(706) 982-5522

www.ingramcontent.com/pod-product-compliance
Lightning Source LLC
Chambersburg PA
CBHW081155040426
42445CB00015B/1895